LANGUAGE-ARTS EXPLORER

AMERICA:
THREE WORLDS
MEET

Beginnings to 1620

by M. J. Cosson

HISTORY DIGS

CHERRY LAKE PUBLISHING • ANN ARBOR, MICHIGAN

CHERRY LAKE

Publishing

Published in the United States of America
by Cherry Lake Publishing
Ann Arbor, Michigan
www.cherrylakepublishing.com

Printed in the United States of America
Corporate Graphics Inc
September 2011
CLFA09

Consultants: Brett Barker, associate professor of history, University of Wisconsin–Marathon County; Gail Saunders-Smith, associate professor of literacy, Beeghly College of Education, Youngstown State University

Editorial direction:
Rebecca Rowell

Design and production:
Marie Tupy

Photo credits: North Wind Picture Archives, cover, 1, 5, 7, 10, 16, 21, 23, 27, 30; Simon van de Passe/Library of Congress, 9; Library of Congress, 12; Mast, Crowell & Kirkpatrick/Library of Congress, 13; Shutterstock Images, 15, 25; John White/Theodor de Bry/Library of Congress, 19; iStockphoto, 24

Library of Congress Cataloging-in-Publication Data
Cosson, M. J.
 America : three worlds meet / by M.J. Cosson.
    p. cm. – (Language Arts Explorer. History digs.)
 Includes bibliographical references and index.
 ISBN 978-1-61080-193-5 – ISBN 978-1-61080-281-9 (pbk.)
 1. America–Discovery and exploration–Juvenile literature. I. Title.
 E101.C797 2011
 973.1–dc23
                               2011015118

Cherry Lake Publishing would like to acknowledge the work of The Partnership for 21st Century Skills. Please visit www.21stCenturySkills.org for more information.

TABLE OF CONTENTS

You are being given a mission. The facts in What You Know will help you accomplish it. Remember the clues from What You Know while you are reading the story. The clues and the story will help you answer the questions at the end of the book. Have fun on this adventure!

YOUR MISSION

Your mission is to learn to think like a historian. What tools do historians use to research the past? What kinds of questions do they ask, and where do they look for answers? On this assignment, your goal is to investigate the historical period from when Christopher Columbus first set foot on American soil to the settlement of Jamestown. Who already lived in the Americas? Who arrived there by crossing the Atlantic Ocean, and why did they travel to the Americas? How did they affect the lives of American Indians? How did Africans end up in North America as slaves? As you investigate, keep in mind What You Know.

WHAT YOU KNOW

★ American Indians had lived in the Americas for thousands of years before Columbus arrived.

★ North America was largely unknown to Europeans.

★ Between 1492 and 1620, explorers and other Europeans began traveling to and settling in North America.

★ Africans were mostly brought to the Americas as **captive** slaves.

Use this book to explore history in ways a historian might. A student is exploring this time in U.S. history with the help of the research team for a documentary film about this era. She is keeping a journal of her discoveries. Carry out your mission by reading the student's journal.

This is one artist's depiction of Columbus standing
on the deck of his ship during his voyage to the Americas.
The journey would change the world.

I spent several days with the research team for *Three Worlds Meet*, a documentary film that is being made. A documentary presents factual information, so everything must be carefully researched. It takes time to get all of the facts right.

The Taíno

My first interview was with Joe. He is researching the lifestyles of American Indians. Joe showed me photographs of artifacts from an **archaeological** site on the Bahamian island of San Salvador. This is where Christopher Columbus and his crew are believed to have met the Taíno people in 1492. It was during his first of four trips to the Americas, which Europeans referred to as the New World.

"These gourds were excavated at the site," Joe said. "The Taíno used them to store food and water, for eating and drinking, as musical instruments, and even as decoys to attract birds."

"I can imagine how they'd be used for most of those things," I said. "But how were they used as decoys?"

"Look here," Joe said, pointing to a drawing of a man catching a bird with his bare hands and what appeared to be a gourd on his head.

"That's interesting," I replied. "The drawing is helpful. Are there any Taíno people you can talk to about their history?"

"Unfortunately, no," Joe responded. "There aren't any left."

Learning from Explorers

Joe explained that a lot of information about the Taíno and other American Indians comes from European explorers' writings.

Columbus and his crew met friendly people in the Caribbean who brought provisions to the Europeans.

On Columbus's second trip, he brought Ramon Pane, who lived with the Taíno and wrote about them. Joe showed me some of Pane's writings that described the Taíno as a peaceful, helpful, and friendly people.

"But the Europeans who came to the New World were cruel to them, especially the Spaniards," Joe said. "They used the Taíno as slaves and worked them hard."

"So, the Spaniards worked them all to death?" I asked. "That's why there aren't any Taíno left?"

"Not quite," Joe explained. "The Taíno eventually died off from illnesses the explorers brought from Europe, such as **smallpox** and **tuberculosis**. The Taíno had never been around those diseases, so they hadn't built up immunity."

That seemed very sad and unfair to me. Joe continued to explain what European explorers did in North America.

"The Englishman Sir Walter Raleigh tried to establish an **outpost** along the Carolina coast," Joe explained. "He brought along people to help him understand the Croatan people he encountered. He asked John White, an artist, mapmaker, and fellow explorer, to record the New World and its inhabitants. White made sketches and paintings of the land, plants, animals, and people. This is his work," Joe said, showing me images of some of White's paintings.

"Why did Raleigh go to all that trouble?" I asked.

DEATH BY DISEASE

When Europeans arrived in the Americas, they brought more than different languages, customs, and dress. They also brought diseases the American Indians had never been exposed to. This and the fact that vaccines hadn't been invented yet meant native peoples such as the Taíno and Croatan were not immune to smallpox and the other diseases the Europeans introduced. As a result, entire groups of people were wiped out, including the Taíno and Croatan.

Sir Walter Raleigh's interest in the New World led to valuable artifacts such as paintings and writings.

"He did it so the people in England could understand what the settlers in the New World were experiencing," Joe said.

I learned that Raleigh also asked his science adviser, Thomas Harriot, to write about the Croatan. Joe explained that a Croatan named Manteo worked with White and Harriot, learning English and helping them learn the Croatan language and way of life.

"So, if Harriot was asked to write about the Croatan, there's a book about them?" I asked.

Joe showed me a copy of Harriot's *Briefe and True Report of the New Found Land of Virginia: of the Commodities and the Nature and Manners of the Natural Inhabitants.*

"These have been great resources," Joe said. "I don't always have this much information about American Indians because they didn't have a written language. Fortunately, some of their history has come down through retellings by the Haudenosaunee, who are also known as the Iroquois. Can you imagine memorizing so much history and passing it orally through several generations?"

"No," I said, shaking my head. Joe continued to tell me about American Indian history.

The Truth about Pocahontas

"There's a lot of misinformation about early American Indians," Joe said, showing me photographs of a small, tattered booklet. "Bishop Bartolomé de Las Casas wrote and argued against Spanish cruelty toward American Indians. The bishop had been the **editor** of Columbus's journal and later became an **advocate** for the American Indians. He spent most of his life arguing for their fair treatment. In 1552, he published the book *The Destruction of the Indies.*"

"Wow," I said. "I'm glad some Europeans were sensitive to the **plight** of American Indians back then."

"But some European accounts may not be accurate," Joe said. "Have you heard of Pocahontas?"

"It's a love story between the Englishman John Smith and Pocahontas, an American Indian," I replied.

"That's what popular culture would have us believe," Joe said. "Actually, when Smith came to

Jamestown in 1607, Pocahontas was only 11 years old. According to Smith's journal, her father, Powhatan, was about to have Smith killed when Pocahontas **intervened** to protect him. Powhatan was an important Indian leader."

"I saw that in a movie," I said.

Joe showed me part of Smith's story about himself:

> *Two great stones were brought before Powhatan: then as many as could laid hands on him, dragged him to them, and thereon laid his head, and being ready with their clubs, to beat out his brains, Pocahontas the King's dearest daughter, when no entreaty would prevail, got his head in her arms, and laid her own upon his to save him from death.*

"Historians now think this might have been a ceremony because they doubt that an Indian girl would defy her father in the way Smith described," Joe explained. "Smith tended to **embellish** his stories. His version could be what really happened, but we don't know who decided it meant Pocahontas was in love with Smith. In fact, she married an English settler named John Rolfe in 1614."

Something my history teacher said earlier in the year clicked. History isn't always told by those who experienced it—sometimes, it takes some digging to get to the facts! ★

My next interview was with Anna, who is investigating explorers. As Anna finds journals, ships' logs, correspondence, and other writing and primary sources for each explorer, she studies that person's achievements. She was still working on Columbus when I met with her.

Finding the New World

"Hi, Anna," I said. "I just learned from Joe about Columbus and other Europeans coming to the New World. Can you tell me why Columbus decided to come here?"

"Sure. Columbus was a businessman who wanted to get rich," Anna explained. "Columbus was Italian. His given name was Cristoforo Colombo. He was an expert navigator who joined Portugal's merchant marine fleet."

"Portugal? But I thought he traveled to the New World for Spain," I said.

Christopher Columbus

This painting shows Columbus discussing his planned journey with Spain's King Ferdinand and Queen Isabella. Without their financial backing, he could not have traveled to the New World.

Anna confirmed that Columbus did, explaining that the explorer first approached King John II of Portugal for financial support for his trip. The king declined, but Columbus later received support from Spain's King Ferdinand and Queen Isabella.

"He took a huge chance, thinking he'd reach the East if he sailed west," Anna said.

"I don't understand what was so important about heading west and finding Asia," I said. "And why would someone travel in the opposite direction of where they really wanted to be?"

COLUMBUS'S CRITICS

Some critics scoffed at Columbus's plans to head west to reach the East. They disagreed with his mathematics about the earth's circumference. The Greek Eratosthenes had accurately estimated the circumference in 250 BCE, and many educated Europeans had a rough idea of this number. Still, Columbus claimed it was thousands of miles less. Given ship technology, Columbus would have died at sea if there had been nothing but ocean between Spain and Asia. That is why he was mocked. Fortunately for Columbus, the Americas existed, so he and his crew didn't die at sea.

"Travelers and traders such as Marco Polo had brought back riches and new resources from the East in the 1300s. Polo's adventures had been written down and rewritten by scribes," Ann explained, showing me photographs of a book handwritten in another language, a type of Italian. "Eventually, many people in Italy knew of Polo's adventures and the riches to be found in the East. Columbus wanted to find a quicker route there."

Leading the Way for Others

Anna said ships and supplies for a long voyage were expensive. Most explorers were paid by royalty to look for new lands, routes, and riches in the name of the country.

"King Ferdinand and Queen Isabella **commissioned** Columbus," Anna said. "This is a copy of a letter Columbus wrote to Luis de Santángel, the king and queen's royal treasurer in 1493. It describes several islands Columbus visited, including one he named La Isla Española, or Hispaniola."

"That's home to Haiti and the Dominican Republic," I declared.

"That's right," Anna confirmed.

I read the letter. It included a description of the island:

Hispaniola is a marvel. Its hills and mountains, fine plains and open country, are rich and fertile for planting and for pasturage, and for building towns and villages. The seaports there are incredibly fine, as also the magnificent rivers, most of which bear gold.

Anna showed me a letter Columbus wrote to the king and queen about his trip and discoveries. In it, he recommended what to do with the island. He suggested that people come and build two or three towns. Columbus's voyage began European colonization of the Americas. I realized one man's idea led to a trip that changed the world. ★

Entry 3: CONQUISTADORES AND PIRATES

When I finished talking to Anna, she introduced me to Henry. His black curly hair, beard, and hoop earring made him look like a pirate. Henry hopes to be one of the pirates in the documentary.

Spanish Explorers

"What do Spanish explorers have to do with pirates?" I asked.

"Pirates have been around as long as recorded history," Henry explained. "A pirate is basically someone who robs others at sea."

He told me Spaniards who explored Mexico, Central America, and South America were called conquistadores. As they conquered the **indigenous** people and took over their empires, the conquistadores stole gold, silver, spices, and other riches to take back to Spain. Henry showed me portraits of conquistadores Francisco Pizarro and Hernán Cortés.

During the mid-1500s, French and English pirates raided Spanish ships laden with **plunder** from the Americas. He showed me an old map of the Caribbean Sea and neighboring waters, including the Gulf of Mexico. The area was labeled the Spanish Main.

"This is where the Spanish ships sailed, and it's where pirates waited for them," he said.

I had always liked pirate movies and was eager to hear more.

Taking Treasures

"A letter of marque was the legal form that allowed pirates known as privateers to go after ships from other countries," Henry explained. "England's Queen Elizabeth I used privateers."

"Kings and queens paid privateers to raid ships of other countries?" I asked.

"Not quite," he said, showing me images of letters of marque he had found online. "Instead, privateers kept some of what they stole."

"Using one ship headed by an able pirate was a lot cheaper for a country than maintaining a big navy," Henry explained.

"So, the monarchs and the privateers let the other country get the riches and then attacked the other country's ship on its way home?" I asked.

When Henry said they did, I shook my head in disbelief. If I hadn't seen the evidence, I might not have believed what he told me. ★

PIRATES STILL EXIST

In the early 2000s, pirates were in the news. Off the coast of Somalia, near the tip of Africa, pirates routinely hijacked ships of all sizes, ranging from yachts to tankers. They often held passengers, crew, and cargo for huge ransoms, sometimes in the millions of dollars. Somali pirates have been known to kill their victims, but this has not been common.

Today, I talked with Franco about the people who inhabited the first colonies. Franco said colonization is when a country sends some of its citizens to live in an unsettled area. By doing so, the country extends its political and economic control over that area.

Strangers in a Strange Land

"I can't imagine what the European explorers must have experienced when they arrived in the Americas," I told Franco. "It really was a new world for them, wasn't it?"

"Think about this," he said. "The first Europeans came into what seemed like a wilderness. It was inspiring to some, including Sir Walter Raleigh. He had tried to start two colonies, but both failed. You can see his optimism in this description he wrote."

Franco showed me some of Raleigh's writing:

> *I never saw a more beautiful country, nor more lively prospects . . . the plains adjoining without bush or stubble, all fair green grass . . . the birds towards the evening singing on every tree . . . cranes and herons of white, crimson, and carnation perching on the river's side, the air fresh with a gentle easterly wind, and every stone that we stooped to take up, promised either gold or silver.*

Franco said a **colony** was finally settled successfully by the English in the early 1600s. But it wasn't easy. When the English

John White captured the lives of the American Indians living in Virginia in his paintings. This group was fishing.

settled Jamestown in the area that is now Chesapeake Bay, Virginia, they encountered the Powhatan. This was a group of several tribes who joined together and were named for a powerful chief, Pocahontas's father. The colonists and the American Indians had a relationship that was both good and bad. The two groups traded. The colonists gave the Powhatan metal tools and other things. In exchange, the American Indians gave the colonists food. But the groups mistrusted each other. Sometimes, there was violence between them, and the Powhatan killed colonists who wandered beyond the English settlement.

"It must have been hard for the groups to learn how to exist with each other," I said. I'm curious, though, to know how the colonists even got to the New World. How did they pay for the trip? I learned from Anna that it was expensive to travel from Europe.

Indentured Servants

"Here's an ad for **indentured servants**," Franco said, showing me a handbill. "Many of the Jamestown settlers who came in 1607 were indentured servants. All they had to do was sign a contract to work for five to seven years for the man who had paid for their passage to America and they could board the ship."

"What were the colonists going to do for work?" I asked.

"Farm," Franco explained. "They were going to grow tobacco and send it back to England. But things didn't go as smoothly as the colonists hoped they would."

Struggling to Survive

Franco showed me a long, beautifully handwritten letter from a Jamestown inhabitant. He condensed what it said for me. "Basically, times were tough," Franco explained. "Most of the first people in

PRESERVING HISTORY

With time, documents and photographs can fade and become brittle. Sometimes, papers fall apart. Preserving original documents is important for keeping accurate historical information. One way to preserve artifacts is to limit handling of them. That's why historians sometimes wear gloves when paging through an old book. This keeps the oils from the person's skin from touching the paper, which can damage it. Another way to preserve history is to digitize it. By scanning documents and photographs, historians create electronic versions of artifacts that can be easily accessed at libraries, museums, and even on the Internet.

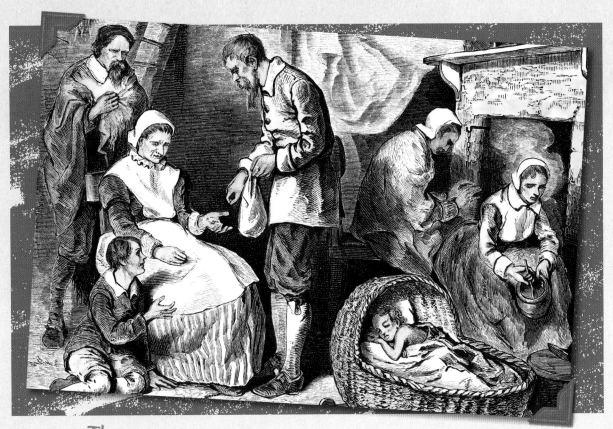

This painting is one artist's version of the starving time. It shows Jamestown colonists passing out their last kernels of corn.

Jamestown died because food was scarce. The colonists called this the starving time. They couldn't produce enough crops to feed themselves, much less extra to send to England."

"How did they survive?" I asked.

"Only the strong made it," Franco said. "Ten tough years went by until they finally managed to send a supply of tobacco to England in 1617. They then needed a sufficient supply of labor to grow and harvest the new crop. At first, they relied on the work of whole families or indentured servants. However, they needed more help, and their solution was inhumane. But I'll let Anna finish the story when you meet with her again tomorrow." ★

On my last day with the research team, I met with Anna again. She had several maps. Some showed routes from Africa to the New World to Europe and back to Africa. Anna said these were the routes slave ships took. I knew about slave ships, but I had never thought about how slavery began. Anna had the answers.

The Beginning of African Enslavement

"Do you remember Franco telling you the colonists needed more labor?" she asked. "That's how slavery began here."

"As the Portuguese and Spanish, especially, continued to explore the African Coast, they came upon treasures in the form of gold, ivory, and human labor," Anna explained. "The western banks of Africa became known as the Ivory Coast, the Gold Coast, and the Slave Coast."

"I don't really see how people compare to ivory and gold," I said.

"The African people lived in tribes, much like the American Indians did," Anna said. "African tribes fought each other for resources and land and sometimes took members of other tribes as prisoners. The leaders of the various tribes in Africa traded their prisoners of war for goods from Europe, such as guns and ammunition."

"Which they probably used to fight the other tribes," I said.

"Exactly," she said.

She said the traded prisoners were taken to the coast, put on slave ships, and taken to the Americas. European slave traders, or slavers, also captured people and put them on ships.

Africans who became enslaved often had been captured by members of other African tribes and sold to slave traders.

Slavery Begins in the Colonies

"In the Americas, sugar cane was the big crop, but it was labor-intensive," Anna explained. "There were other crops, too, such as rice and tobacco. The colonists and new plantation owners needed more labor. The American Indians were difficult to coerce through slavery. It was too easy for them to fight or run away. And many native peoples died from the diseases brought by the Europeans."

"That's why the colonists turned to African slavery," I said.

Anna said it was and explained that enslaved people were treated horribly. "They were beaten, chained, crammed into the ships, and fed poorly," she said. "A huge number of people died on the journey to the coast and then across the sea. More slaves died of **scurvy** and other illnesses later from improper nutrition and poor sanitation on the ships."

Anna told me a Dutch ship robbed a Spanish ship of 20 slaves in 1619 and took them to Jamestown where they were sold. These Africans were the first slaves in Jamestown.

"During this early period, African slaves were treated about the same as indentured servants," Anna explained. "But that changed as slavery became more popular with the colonists. In only a few decades, the Europeans and colonists would develop a trade system that would last almost 300 years and affect millions of Africans by enslaving them. That's not part of our documentary, but it's an important part of our history."

THE TRIANGULAR TRADE ROUTE

The delivery of 20 African slaves to Jamestown in 1619 marked the beginning of slavery in the colony and created the triangular trade route. In Africa, people were captured and traded to slavers in exchange for European goods. The captives were shipped to the Americas. There, they were traded for goods such as sugar, cotton, tobacco, ginger, molasses, and pearls, which went to European countries. Then, the triangle started again. It was the largest forced movement of humans in history.

A memorial in Africa shows the inhumane treatment slaves often experienced.

My week with the *Three Worlds Meet* crew is up. I've learned so much about early American history and the valuable resources available to researchers. I've also seen the importance of accuracy when making a documentary. I look forward to seeing the film when it comes out. ★

MISSION ACCOMPLISHED!

Congratulations! You learned about Christopher Columbus arriving in the Americas and how this launched an era of exploration and settlement. You read about how explorers and settlers affected American Indians, including how some tribes were completely wiped out by diseases brought from Europe. You discovered that pirates really existed. You also learned how Africans were enslaved and brought to North America. Good job!

CONSIDER THIS

★ Put yourself in the place of the American Indians who lived when North America was first explored and settled. How would you feel if strangers moved to your town and began to change everything? How would you respond?

★ What are three differences you see between how people were treated in the fifteenth century and how they are treated today? What does this say about human rights?

★ How could the early colonists have cultivated their crops without the help of slaves? How would this have changed history?

This map shows the Jamestown settlement. The success of Jamestown started colonization that led to the founding of the United States.

GLOSSARY

advocate (AD-vuh-kit) someone who supports or intercedes to help another person or group

archaeological (ahr-kee-uh-LAH-ji-kuhl) about the study of ancient cultures through tools and other artifacts

captive (KAP-tiv) a person held as a prisoner

circumference (sur-KUM-fuh-uhns) the distance around something, such as the globe

editor (ED-i-tur) a person who corrects writing

embellish (em-BEL-ish) to make something more interesting through enhancement, decoration, or exaggeration

indentured servant (in-DENT-churd SUR-vuhnt) a person who has signed a contract to work for someone for a specific amount of time

indigenous (in-DIJ-uh-nuhs) native or original to a place

intervene (in-tur-VEEN) to interfere

outpost (OUT-pohst) a settlement in a remote area

plunder (PLUHN-dur) riches and goods stolen from another

scurvy (SKUR-vee) a disease caused by not getting enough vitamin C

smallpox (SMAWL-pahks) a very contagious disease that causes a high fever, headache, and blisters that may result in scars

tuberculosis (tu-bur-kyuh-LOH-sis) a very contagious disease that affects the lungs

LEARN MORE

BOOKS

Aller, Susan Bivin. *Christopher Columbus*. Minneapolis, MN:
 Lerner, 2003.

Freedman, Russell. *Who Was First? Discovering the Americas*.
 New York, NY: Clarion Books, 2007.

Kramer, Sydelle. *Who Was Ferdinand Magellan?* New York:
 Grosset & Dunlap, 2004.

Ward, Nancy. *Sir Walter Raleigh: Founding the Virginia Colony*.
 New York: Crabtree, 2006.

WEB SITES

Africans in America: The Terrible Transformation
http://www.pbs.org/wgbh/aia/part1/narrative.html
 Learn how Africans were brought to North America.

Conquistadores
http://www.pbs.org/opb/conquistadors/home.htm
 This PBS site provides information about conquistadores in the
 Americas, including a timeline of their conquest.

Jamestown Settlement
http://historyisfun.org/Jamestown-Settlement.htm
 Tour this living history museum online. Information includes a
 timeline, kids' museum guides, and videos.

FURTHER MISSIONS

MISSION 1

Sailing ships were the mode of transportation for all immigrants to the New World. Use books and the internet to learn more about sailing ships of the fifteenth and sixteenth centuries. Next, compare crossing the Atlantic Ocean today with crossing it when Columbus did. What transportation is used today? How long does it take? How do the trips differ?

MISSION 2

Explorers, scientists, mathematicians, musicians, theologians, and artists all were making new discoveries and breaking boundaries during this period. Imagine you are someone from this period. If you are an inventor, describe your invention. How might it help people and change the world? If you are an explorer like Columbus and need money, write a letter to the person you want to commission you. Then, pretend you receive the commission and record an entry in your journal about what you have seen on your travels.

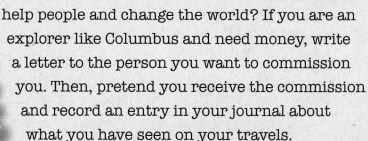

ABOUT THE AUTHOR

M. J. Cosson holds an MEd, has taught art, and has written many children's fiction and nonfiction books. She lives in the Texas hill country with her husband, dogs, cat, and occasional visiting grandchildren.

ABOUT THE CONSULTANTS

Brett Barker is an associate professor of history at the University of Wisconsin-Marathon County in Wausau. He received his PhD in history from the University of Wisconsin-Madison and his MA and BA in history from Ohio State University. He has worked with K-12 teachers in two Teaching American History grants.

Gail Saunders-Smith is a former classroom teacher and Reading Recovery teacher leader. Currently, she teaches literacy courses at Youngstown State University in Ohio. Gail is the author of many books for children and three professional books for teachers.